In Her Shoes: Single Parent Volume 2

Co-authored by:

Bianca Piper

Carla Shelton

Marlee Mauvis

Yamaceeta Thompson

Francoise Isaac

Carolyn David-Graves

In Her Shoes: Single Parent Volume 2
Copyright © 2018 by UImpact Publishing
All Rights Reserved.

No part of this book may be used, reproduced, uploaded, stored or introduced into a retrieval system, or transmitted in any way or by any means (including electronic, mechanical, recording, or otherwise), without the prior written permission of the publisher, with the exception of brief quotations for written reviews or articles. No copying, uploading, or distribution of this book via the Internet is permissible.

The author, writers, and publisher have made every effort to include accurate information and website addresses in this work at the time of publication, and assume no responsibility for changes, omissions, inaccuracies, or errors that occur before or after publication. The publisher does not endorse or assume responsibility for information, author and writer websites, or third-party websites, or their content.

In Her Shoes: Single Parent Volume 2

ISBN-13: 978-1729561119

ISBN-10: 172956111X

TABLE OF CONTENTS

Bianca Piper
-5-

Carla Shelton
-17-

Marlee Mauvis
-33-

Yamaceeta Thompson
-53-

Francoise Isaac
-63-

Carolyn David-Graves
-85-

BIANCA PIPER

When did you realize you would be a single parent, what was your initial response?

I remember it like it was yesterday. Being eighteen, scared, deep down knowing that something was different. I thought it was something temporary going on. I never dreamed of being pregnant. I took a test and it was positive. I couldn't believe what I was seeing. This was one of the scariest moments in my life. How can I get out of this? I'm too young for this. All these thoughts went through my head. I was in utter disbelief. I was in a relationship at the time with the father. He was very supportive. After going back and forth in my head, whether to abort, or parent; I decided to parent. I just started college and was in a "puppy love" situation so every time I felt defeated I started to think "maybe it will be better if I just got rid of this situation all together." By the grace of God, I stuck it out and on February 19, 2010, I became a 19-year-old mother of a girl I named Kailey Rynee' Fuller. I named her after one of my family members who passed away as a child. Although her name was very special to me, that moment wasn't. I didn't feel connected, I just knew that my life was going to change drastically.

Over the course of three years, it was rough. Between having to "become adults," pressure to get married, and a child, things got too hard for us to deal with. We constantly fought over money and misunderstandings. After being together for four years, we decided to part ways and raise Kailey in separate homes. Another devastating blow, as I never wanted this for my daughter. Disconnected is the best way I could describe what I felt about Kailey the first three to four years of her life. She was a wonderful kid, I was just so overwhelmed with life that I wanted to check out and give up.

Here we are, two babies, living in this big world. I didn't have a clue what it meant to parent. All I know is that I had to keep this kid alive! This season was also hard because exchanges with Kailey's dad were so difficult for my soul. Every time I walked away feeling defeated. Suddenly, when Kailey turned about 4 years old, I was extremely depressed, but something went off in my head. It went like "Bianca, your daughter deserves so much more than you have given her, don't you want to be different?" I answered, "YES, YES, she didn't ask to be here, so I need to get better for her!" I tried anti-depressants and they made me feel really numb. So, numb that others around me noticed. That wasn't helpful in what I was trying to accomplish so I felt stuck and hoped for a life change.

I met a lady who asked me if I knew Jesus. I told her I did but also told her parts of my broken story. She invited me to a biblical 12 step program. During this program, Jesus got ahold of my heart and started to transform me, just like I was hoping for. Things didn't suddenly become a breeze. In fact, things became harder. I had to think much more than I had to before. I had to be more intentional and think through my decisions as a believer. At this time, I was 23, afraid still, but knew that there was more to life.

What kind of support systems do you have in place?

Praise God for friends, right!? I was working for a gynecologist at the time and she was (and still is) one of my biggest cheerleaders. I made many friends the 5 years I worked in that office. Friends who would pick Kailey up for me. Friends who would pray for us, feed us, love on Kailey when I couldn't. This really helped me to understand God's love for us. His unconditional, kind, and selfless love for me and my baby girl. I started to feel as though life is coming back together and there might be some good in being a single parent. Society tells you that this is a burden and an unfortunate situation but never speaks to the upside of things. I was starting to feel the slightest bit of hope! I ended up getting baptized and after doing this, I made the conscious decision to try to be what Kailey needed me to be. I knew I was still broken but I didn't want to give up as easily as I had in the past. This is when darkness wasn't at controlling my life any longer.

Life for us looks different obviously as we grow physically but also emotionally and spiritually. My big girl is now 8 years old, she is in 2nd grade and thriving! I remember thinking, we were not a family unless we have a man, woman, and kids. Today, I don't believe this to be true. Kailey and I are a family. A whole one! It truly takes a village to raise kids. Single parent or not, parenting is a lot of work, and it takes many hands, feet, and hearts. I love to look back and see what God has done to support my family. So many of my personal friendships were built on willingness to help with my daughter. For example, right now, once a week one of my friends picks Kailey up for me so I can attend biblical counseling. Kailey is in school and needs to be in bed at a reasonable hour. So, for me to thrive as a mom, and her to thrive as a student, my friends step in and help! Her dad, aunts, and grandparents also help us. Mom guilt does set in when I can't be at every event, every class party, or sit down for every homework assignment. I am here to tell you, let others help you. You are only one person and you can't get it all in alone. For me, that looks like my sister going to a Valentine's Day party, or my mom going to get muffins with moms. My heart desires to be at those things, but I just can't and work a full-time job AND stay sane! Ha-ha!

What does work/life balance look like for you? How do you find a rhythm?

Another obstacle of parenting is being able to provide for your kids. For most of us that looks like us having to work a fulltime job. My biggest takeaway from this part of my life is to plan. Keep a calendar. Of course, things don't always go as planned BUT a calendar will help to physically see what needs to be done by when. It can also help you to visualize what that week can look like. Whether to plan for a busy week with quick meals or thoughtful meals due to a slower week. With work, kids' activities and school, this can be a HUGE help. It is great to have a community behind you because at least one night a week, someone else is preparing a meal for us. Whether it's a friend picking Kailey up then we just eat at their house, or a friend bringing us a meal, that one meal takes a lot of the load from me as a single parent. Also, it is important for me to keep a job that is understanding. Since I became a mom I always informed my supervisors that I have a daughter, and they have been supportive. My work/home balance is sometimes all over the place. Some weeks we are only home two nights a week and some weeks we are home all week. I doubt I'll find a constant rhythm in this season of life. However, there is a lot of love and time spent together. At times this looks like us eating dinner in a parked car before we get to our destination just so I can slow down and ask my daughter how her day was.

How have you pursued your goals and dreams despite being a single parent?

Over the past eight years I have been in survival mode in various aspects. Financially, emotionally, mentally—all the things you can think of. I became a mom so young that I never had time to think about my purpose or what to do next. Once Jesus came into my life, I realized everything I've gone through, is for good and for His glory. This to me means using the life He has put before me to build up His Kingdom and create disciples. What does that mean? In this season it means loving on the moms that I work with through their pregnancies. That looks like loving and serving my coworkers. I love and serve my home, my friends, and people who I don't even know. Purpose for me right now is to love others well. In loving others, I started Soul of a Single Mama. It's a social media site and email group that caters to encouraging single parents in their walk as a parent who seeks God and the hearts of their kids. I haven't quite grasped what I want to do as a long-time career, but I do pray the Lord can be seen in what I'm doing currently.

What is your biggest challenge/biggest joy in parenting?

Parenting for me, is a joy. I love the challenges we overcome. I love the stepping stones we have all around that remind us of God's love for us. I think the most joyful thing currently about being a mom is getting to see Kailey grow. She is such a gracious, fun, and comical girl. Seeing her brain process things and ask questions when she doesn't understand grows our bond every single day. She is very independent and makes wise choices. Even when her choices aren't the wisest, she is aware, and she knows we can talk through them and that there is grace in all situations. This is huge for us now. As far as challenges, I really struggle with overthinking or trying to control situations to make Kailey comfortable. Let's be honest, this world brings no comfort whatsoever, so I'm kind of instilling in her a false hope that the real world will be easy. We tend to take the easiest way out since it is just one of us. For example, when I'm cooking and cleaning, I am quick to put her in front of screen, so she can be out of my way and that seems simple to me. I am not engaging her in the things that will matter down the road. I am learning that I should engage with her and make chores a time for us to interact. We should serve our home together as a family versus me doing all the work. This is where a lot of my sense of being overwhelmed comes from. Doing EVERYTHING alone and I just CANNOT!

Any parenting hacks, or books, or resources you may know about?

I know this may sound cheesy but my biggest book to go to would be The Bible. To me, it's like a how to book. It speaks to the love of God, but how to live a life fulfilled while on earth. I love that. I also believe that biblical counseling is a HUGE tool. Society tells us counseling is more of a go to when you are in crisis mode but that is so not true. Counseling for me has been a person who doesn't know me, so their opinion is unbiased pointing out the lies I am believing on this journey and showing me truth. This has been huge for me especially in the parenting life. My hope for this season of counseling is that I gain a greater knowledge about the lies I've believed, so that I can start off with truth in my household. This is God's grace alone that I can go and process and pour out the most I have into being a mom. A fully aware and intentional mom. Also, like I stated earlier, I started Soul of a Single Mama. It's an emailing list and a social media based source of encouragement for single parents. This is where my heart is now.

How do you infuse self-care in your life?

Self-care for me looks like doing the things that I love. As much as I'd love to say it's a mani/pedi or a massage, LOL, its just not. I love to read and write. These are things I do that don't require a babysitter and I can do in my home. Writing and reading for my soul helps me to process things and internalize the things I may let slip my brain daily. I believe more in soul care than physicality. Physical looks are important, and I love to do nice things for myself, but if I am honest, I just do the bare minimum day to day and focus more on the fruits or not so fruitful aspects of my soul daily. I desire to become better at the things that make me feel like a pretty girl. Once, I get over some hurdles I'll have more insight on that! Serving is also a huge part of my soul care. I serve at my local church on Wednesdays and it brings my soul so much joy. It is truly incredible to get to be apart of that. At times when I must miss out I totally can tell the difference in my week, so I try to make this a part of the MUST DO things on my agenda.

What advice would you give someone who finds themselves in this situation?

THERE IS HOPE! I would never discredit the hardness, bitterness, and anger that comes with being a single parent. It is hard, but we don't have to stay in that place of resentment. Our kids may not be the typical two-parent home kids, but they will be ok if we keep trying. Keep pursuing them even when it doesn't feel good. Give them a safe place to come talk about whatever, and in times where we just can't be everywhere, build community. Build a community of people who will come alongside you and are willing to fill in the gaps when you just can't. Find a church home to get you and your kids plugged into so they can serve others and not hone in on what they lack in their home. This seems to give Kailey some sense of purpose when she is needed to help at our church. Also, I'd say to show yourself lots of grace. Single parent or not, we won't always get it right. Sometimes we may have to apologize, but that is just apart of being a flawed human being. This may kind of be a touchy subject, but I do feel led to say, culturally, being a single parent is very common. Unfortunately, the way we let our view of the other parent affect us can sometimes rub off on our kids. In this, I've learned that ultimately, Kailey's dad and I love her. We both want similar things for her life. Even though they may not line up completely, at the base of it all is love. So, in my frustration, I watch my words and actions around Kailey. I would hate for her to view her dad in a negative light because of something minor that frustrated me. Overall, we have a good relationship. We are just two humans trying to parent in separate households and it is hard to do that. This may not be the case for you, but this is a common scenario I have seen and had to work on since being a single mom for six years.

How have you grown personally as a single parent? How do you think it has affected your kids?

I have grown because I was eighteen when I first became a mom. Deeper than that though, my heart has become softer, I am more understanding, but I am also self-aware. I can read into my heart and actions and try to quickly ask God for grace to remove me from that place. I can say that I am more intentional with Kailey and others I have a relationship with. I try to understand the heart behind other people's responses to me and see where I can understand others more. I've never done any of this or even had the desire to do before becoming a single parent. I have grown in the area of pride. I realize that I can not do everything on my own, but also that is not the way God intended it to be. He intended for us to come alongside one another receive help as His provision for us. As far as Kailey, it has created security in her. She knows her relationship with me is a safe place and that all things I do or don't do are purely out of my love for Jesus and her. She in turn loves others as well and seeks out the hearts of her friends. She is very intentional as well. Kailey knows our home looks different than those around us, but she has this underlying confidence that this is God's best for us in this current season. In all honesty, our life doesn't really have a rhythm or a set way of doing things, but there is a lot of love. Knowing that kids are so resilient has been a huge reminder for me to just do the best I can. That is all that is asked of me. It'll never look perfect, I'll never get it all the way right but if I have tried and not given up, that is what matters most!

BIANCA PIPER

My name is Bianca Piper, and I was born in Dallas, Texas but spent most of my life in a small town called Desoto. That is where I call home. I currently reside in Frisco, Texas. I have an eight-year old daughter who is such a joy. Her name is Kailey! She is in 2nd grade.

I first became a single parent in July of 2012. This has been the most challenging, intentional, rough, encouraging, hopeful, and gracious time in both of our lives. We found Jesus! Also, overall contentment has come in this season of life. Some fun facts about us are, my all time favorite thing to do is write. I am obsessed with words. Now I have passed this trait on to my daughter. Reading is her thing so we bond over words and things we read. I can't wait to share my journey with you!

CARLA SHELTON

Tell us a little about yourself.

My name is Carla and I am a 56-year-old single mother. I love being a mom. It's the hardest job on this earth and yet the most rewarding job one could have. I had my daughter 37 years ago in August and her name is Tracella. My wonderful baby girl came out with this beautiful purple hue to her lovely dark brown skin, I've never seen anything like it. She was so beautiful. But I knew that purple hue was the 'black people' version of asphyxiation. I later learned the umbilical cord was wrapped around her neck and she was moments from death. She has disability challenges that we have learned to just roll with. I also have a son who is now 33 years old. At 6'5, he's striking and commands attention without wanting it. He's married to a beautiful woman and I have a grandson. They are both well.

When I was 36 years old I earned my BFA in Speech Communication/Organizational Management from the former Southwest Texas State University. For the last 14 years I have been a human resource professional. Currently, I am semi-retired as a consultant in HR.

My children were my motivation to keep moving. I just couldn't stop because if I did, they would to. My motto at the time was "I refuse to be a statistic." A young black single mother who's going to end up on the system. Back in the day, this is all that was highlighted in the news and throughout the black community. It even came up in one of my college courses. The stereotype that was prevalent then made any single mother of color want to not try and give up. My children raised me to be what I am today. I am a black, accomplished, middle aged, gray haired, world traveled, happy, believer and let's not forget "dating," beautiful single woman today and loving every minute of life. I honor my children for the sacrifices they made for me and I thank them from the bottom of my heart for loving me enough to not recognize that their mother and father was the same person.

When you realized single parenting was going to be part of your story, what was your initial response?

It's funny, I never thought about being a single mother even when my ex-husband and I were separating. When you're married with kids, sure you do family things together, but when it comes to the kids, the woman is usually the nurturer and caregiver. The woman is the multi-tasker. She gets the kids up and ready for school, takes them to school, goes to work, hurries home to take the kids to their baseball or ballet lessons, goes home, cooks dinner, goes to choir rehearsal, comes home, puts the kids in the tub, tucks them in, and then flops on the bed fully clothed and crashes, sleeps, out like a light. So, when we were splitting up, being a single parent never crossed my mind. I guess subconsciously, I was already a single parent. What was profound to me was that the children wouldn't have their father around. And they loved their dad. He played with them and made them laugh. They would run to him as he was sitting on the couch watching TV to give him a kiss good night.

Being a single parent didn't really hit me until my children got older. When my son was around 10-11 years old he was becoming a teenager and I didn't quite know what to do with his reactions to things, like discipline or show of affection. He always played around and wrestled like most boys. It was then I realized that I was a single parent who had to raise a man without a man. It's funny, the things I didn't know, and I had three brothers! For example, a few years earlier, I had a friend who was a single mother of two boys. I'll call her Karen. Karen's boys, I'll call them Ben and Ken, were about three years older than my kids. Ben, the oldest was 11 years old. Our children became good friends and got along well. One day Karen called me frantic because she couldn't find Ben; Ben ran away. She shared that they had an argument over something simple that Ben didn't want to do, and he ran off and hadn't come home and it had been about two hours. I gathered up the kids and drove over as quickly as I could so I could help her look for Ben. When I got there, Ben had come home. He was crying. She was crying. Everyone was crying! Ben was always a level-headed boy. He never started any trouble, and he made it his job to be the protector of the younger kids. I didn't understand what happened to make him leave like that. I didn't think of relating it to Anthony like that–at least not yet.

The incident bothered me so much I called my brother, who was a soldier in the army to tell him what happened. My brother didn't get excited or act upset at all. I was upset, but he said, "Yeah, he's probably starting to go through puberty." I said, "What are you talking about? Boys don't go through puberty, only girls do." He said, "No, Car (my nickname to the siblings) boys go through puberty too. They can start around 10 years old." I was shocked and speechlessness. He said, "Yes, Anthony will go through it too." When I found my voice, I asked what should I expect? What should I do?

Love my brother. He just laid it out for me. He told me that boys seem to become more immature, their bodies are preparing to change, and it's usually when wet dreams start. He told me I should talk to Anthony about that and tell him it's ok. "We've already talked about sex. I wanted the kids to hear the truth from me. They'll get enough from their friends as they get older. So we started having Q&A sessions about sex a while ago," I said. "Good," my brother said. "That will probably stop because Anthony will start getting embarrassed talking about that stuff with his mother. But if he ever needs to talk, or you want me to talk to him, just give me a call. Oh, and make sure he plays a lot outside. Boys have a lot of energy, anyways, but think more and he'll be tired more too as he gets older."

So, boys go through a physical as well as mental change. I was floored. Where was his dad when I needed him; or better yet, when Anthony needed him? I instantly got angry at my ex. Then I realized that I don't have time for that. I needed to be prepared to get this boy through puberty. Then I felt sad for my son and sad for myself because, bless Anthony's heart, I didn't know. Being a woman, having been a girl, I know how to raise a girl into a young lady, but really had no clue about boys. I began to wonder what I've missed already with him. I thought I've already messed up my son, not knowing his needs for the last five years of his life. He was eight now and getting close to puberty and I couldn't afford to have the pity party. That "bad mother" guilt is going to have to wait until later. That's what we do as single parents. We don't allow ourselves that time to grieve our mistakes.

They say it takes a village to raise a child. What kind of support systems do you have in place?

Support are so important. How do you keep your balance when you are trying to survive and live life as an adult and raise kids single handedly? It's a juggle. A support system could be anyone in your family, in your neighborhood, from your church, or seasoned women that God puts in your life. I was in San Antonio, TX when my kids were elementary school age, from the ages of four to 12. I didn't have family members that were close by. My biggest support was a 78-year-old woman named "Nanny." Her real name was Maggie. She was my savior on earth at the time. I was referred to her when my after-school babysitter, Ms. Brown, couldn't babysit anymore. Nanny loved children. She was the "little old woman who lived in the shoe." She would keep neighborhood kids for days at a time because their mothers were on drugs and the they wanted their child to be safe. So, my kids always had other children to play with at Nanny's house. Nanny was my "weekend" babysitter. Because of Nanny I was finally able to do grown up things.

Single parents are still adults and need to be treated as such. Sometimes, we get caught up in raising the kids that we forget our basic needs and put them on the back burner. This is not just a single mother thing, but a parent thing too. I was in my late 20's and had to figure out how to have a life so that I could stay sane. I hadn't watched a grownup movie for about three years. It's funny how exciting it is when you finally go to a movie that's rated R. I remember being so excited. Nanny baby sat, of course. If I went out on Friday night, Nanny would say, "Don't come back tonight and wake these 'cheeren' up. You come in the morning an' get' em." She literally saved my life. I was able to have a social life and still provide time for my kids.

I wanted my kids to know God and I thought taking them to church was the best way to teach them. We joined this church and the minute we walked in the members embraced us with so much love and care. Both my son and daughter learned so much from all of them. They learned individuality and their talents started to show. For example, my daughter has a cognitive disability and the church wanted to recruit her to be an acolyte (someone who lights the candles at the alter before the service). I automatically said, "no way." I didn't want to be responsible for burning down the church. I told them if you put a stick with fire on the end of it in Tracella's hand, that's surely what's going to happen. But this "village" member encouraged me to let her try and that she will be fine. Tracella was the best little acolyte they had. She did the job with pride for years. It was always fun for Tracella. She never grew out of the task.

Work/Life balance. What does that look like for you, and how did you find your rhythm?

As a single parent I had to find balance in not only work but in my life as well. When a parent puts the kids first you find a way to incorporate and be with them. Church is a prime example of this. Anthony and Tracella were in everything kid related at the church; choir, Sunday school, kid's bible study, vacation bible school and whatever event came up for kids. What was great is that I became a part of everything they did. I assisted the children's choir, I taught Sunday school and vacation bible school. That was a good way to have quality time with them and be involved without it taking time away from them, especially working a 9-5.

I enrolled my son in baseball when he was seven. My daughter was 11 and was running track in the Special Olympics. Well, the opening game and parade of the season was on the same day that Tracella was running in the Special Olympics. I knew this was happening a few weeks before, and I was frantic as to how I was going to pull off being in both places. I couldn't be in two places at once. So, my mom flew from Arizona to Texas to go and watch my son play baseball, and I went to the Special Olympics with my daughter. It was a busy day, but we made it through. What a blessing my mom was that day.

When my son was in high school he played baseball and games started at 3 p.m. My boss (another village member) knew that I worked hard, put in extra time either by staying late or coming in early some days so that I could go to my son's sports activities during the week. I believe in his high school years I only missed two games. Letting the people around you know your story helps. You can't be shy or embarrassed about your life. I made sure everyone I worked with at each job since the kids were born knew them and knew my walk of life. They don't need to know all the private details but enough to understand, accept, and be patient with me.

Often you hear that being a single parent means you have to sacrifice your dreams and goals?

I believe that it's not so much that I sacrificed my goals and dreams, but that I didn't think I could make them happen because I didn't have the time with working. I always thought the kids would just roll with what's going on. Sometimes we're so dedicated to the thought of surviving and caring for the kids that you get tunnel vision and forget to look out of the box. I believe you can do anything with your kids. Kids are very resilient. You just throw them on your back like swans and keep going.

I did not have my degree and wanted so much to go back to school. I decided to try to attend a university and see if I could get accepted and the money to pay for school. I applied for financial aid and got everything and more. The extra I received from financial aid was through a program that was specifically for "single mothers." Financial aid gave me an extra thousand dollars a semester. I didn't know that there was such a grant. But I never would have known if I did't try to go back to school. My financial aid was enough to pay for school, books and for my living expense if I budgeted well. I also tried and applied to state agencies. I applied for a housing program called "Self Sufficiency" and finally got on in by my 2nd semester. This gave me reduced housing and let me build equity at the same time. This support enabled me to stop working full-time and move to a weekend job. Everything is possible. I had a lot of foolish pride at the time. But I decided to lighten my load and get rid of it. My life became so much better once the pride was gone.

Once I got over the fear of 'how do I feed my kids while going to school', it all worked out. My first two years I went to school on Tuesdays and Thursdays only. I was able to be room mom for my son's class. What a difference it made in his behavior, both at school and at home. He settled down and started to be better at school and listened more at home. The last two years of college I had to be at the campus everyday for the upper level courses. I started having weekend exams and most times I didn't have a babysitter. So, I took my kids to school with me. I had a class that was in this big auditorium. On exam day, I put Tracella and Anthony, with color books at the top of the auditorium where no one was sitting, and they were quiet the whole time. The problem is I couldn't give 100% to the exam, because I had half my brain on them and the other half on the test. The BFA is as much their degree as it is mine.

How have you pursued your dreams and goals despite being a single parent?

It takes a village and you say "yes". Yes, I graduated from a university. I got into a corporate job in Alaska. I was able to travel for the company all over the United States and internationally. Just liked I dreamed I wanted to do. I wanted a job where they would aid paid for my travel because I wanted to travel, and I didn't think I would be able to because of the kids. But God made a way and answered that dream. It was awesome. My brother and sister-in-law allowed me to do that. They were my village at the time in Alaska. My older brother lived nearby, and I was able to say "yes." You must pursue your dreams. If you don't then you lose hope, and hope is what carries you through.

What has been your biggest challenge and greatest joy while single parenting?

One of my biggest challenges being a single parent is carrying everything all by myself. Not having that other person to bounce things off. Not having that other person when you have a "good cop, bad cop" moment with your teenager. Not having that other person when you must be in two places at one time and both places are very important.

My son and daughter are very different in personality from each other. My daughter is developmentally delayed and couldn't keep up with her brother who was four years younger. She couldn't speak well, so understanding her really took some time. There were a lot of daily activities that she couldn't do so others had to help her or do them for her. She is very sweet and gentle and loves to laugh at anything. She couldn't discern what was funny and what wasn't. On the other hand, there's my son. Like all boys, he was a ball of energy. He always wanted to play, to explore where ever he was. When he was about five years old, he got the chicken pox and couldn't go to school for a week. I couldn't find anyone who would keep him because no one wanted to handle his energy level. Either way, the single mother guilt started to catch up with me, and I felt I wasn't giving them the kind of attention they needed because I couldn't split myself down the middle. It's mentally and physically exhausting and challenging.

When my son reached seven or eight years old, I decided that it wouldn't hurt them to take them out of school one day every couple of months. I would keep Anthony home from school on the days I would do maintenance things like taking the car for a tune up or I had to go to a Home Depot type store or automotive shop. Then after the chores were done I would take him to McDonalds and we'd take the food to the park. I would find a picnic table and have my book and let him play with the toys or watch him run around with other children until it was time to go pick Tracella up from school. Then I would do the same for Tracella. But with her we would go to a movie or shopping at the mall. But the good thing about this is that I was able to give my undivided attention to each child. They were always excited about their unshared time. They loved school, but I thought the sacrifice of the "perfect attendance" certificate was worth it. Being a parent isn't easy, but being a single parent is harder. But I loved every minute of it. The greatest joy of single parenting is being a parent. The joy of watching your child's personality grow just can't be beat.

Do you have any single parenting hacks, books, or resources other single parents need to know about? We live in a busy, rushed culture. How do you infuse self-care into your life?

I like to read and was always looking for new ideas for whatever I was trying to do. Even the times I felt overwhelmed or down in the dumps I would go find a self-help book for what I needed at that time. I was given a book called *Sacred Pampering Principles* by Debrena Jackson-Gandy. It was awesome. It inspired and taught me how to treat myself better. My book is well worn. I studied it, highlighted probably on every page, and read it several times. This book helped with my hard life and then taught me how to soften it and re-energize it. It told me that although I'm this woman trying to survive with children, I'm also a women who deserves some attention. I felt so much better. We must as women do these things for ourselves. Most single parents can't afford gifts like massages or relaxation excursions. But a self-help book about self-care can go a long way. This book brought balance to me.

Although my children are grown and on their own, I still like a good book on self-care. It centers me in this busy world.

I have since met Debrena Jackson-Gandy and she is a wonderful woman. The biggest advocate for women and self-care one could ever meet. And she is so positive and it's contagious. That helps too. Surround yourself with positive people. People who believe in self-care. I must work at keeping self-care it on my radar, so I don't get burned out. It's worth every effort.

What advice would you give someone who finds themselves in a single parent situation?

I would tell them to throw those kids on your back and keep going. Whatever one wants to do they can do it. Becoming a single parent might delay things but, should never stop what you want to do in your life. Eventually the kids grow up and start making their own decisions without you. Also, create your village. A village is diverse, all colors, races, gender, age, religions, and from all walks of life. Remember a village is fluid. It changes with every phase of the child's life and of the parent's life as well. But a village is what's going to help a single parent keep their dreams alive. My village consist of my family, church members, school workers, my co-workers, friends, coaches.

A quick story. My daughter is developmentally disabled. But when she turned 21, she knew she was an adult and should be living in her own place. I got her an apartment right across the parking lot of my work. She could walk over if she needed anything. There were three ladies in my office with me, and they all knew Tracella. I gave each one of those ladies a key to Tracella's apartment, just in case she got locked out of her house and she had to walked over to my office and I wasn't there. They would be able to give her a key. She locked herself out several times. My village members at that time were those co-workers. I thank God for those three ladies. Single parents, create your village. It could look like anything.

How have you grown personally as a single parent, and what kind of influence do you think that has on your child(ren)?

My children are 33 and 37 years old. "I did it. I made it through." My son is married and has a son, but when he talks about taking care of his "family," I know it includes his sister and me. It makes me so proud. My son saw me as a strong woman and thinks that is what all women should be like. I disagree. I wish I had shown my children more vulnerability because that's what's in real life and real people. But sometimes as single parents we don't have time, don't want to show or admit to vulnerability because of our children. For me, to show vulnerability took away from my "survivability." This was my warped sense of subconscious strength. If I fall, then my kids will fall with me, and I couldn't let that happen.

I can't stand the term Superwoman because when folks call you that, it means all they see is a woman who can do it all with no problems; a single parent household making it with no hiccups, and the children are happy and well adjusted. Then they think she doesn't need help, she's doing just fine because she's Superwoman.

But NO! Single parents have the same needs as married parents. We are vulnerable (I just couldn't afford to put this word in my vocabulary) and need help. Whether it's someone telling your child to stop being bad, or teaching your son how to groom himself like a man instead of a woman 'cause that's all mom knew how to do, or teaching your son how to be a man, we do our best as single parents. And I give all single parents, and myself, kudos. But when your kids grow up, you see the cracks of your parenting because of the light shining through them and you're like, "Oh shoot, I didn't even think about that part of teaching or parenting. And it's a big gap too." Most parents could say this. But I keep praying for my children and for God to give them what I didn't know or forgot.

My experiences as a single parent are what made me who I am today, and I'm better for it.

CARLA SHELTON

My name is Carla Shelton and I have two children. My daughter, Tracella is 38 and has special needs. My son Anthony is 33, and ready to take over the world. I am a graduate of Texas State University with a Bachelor of Arts degree. I then moved to Alaska where I entered the corporate world just where I thought my degree would take me. I believe in giving back to the community, because the community gave to me when I needed it. I was on the Alaska YWCA board for six years. I was on the Governor's Council in two states as an advocate for the disabled community. God is the rock I stand on. He has blessed me over the years with food on our plates and money in the mail. Being a single parent isn't ideal, but one could raise happy kids and give them everything they need.

MARLEE MAUVIS

Tell us a little about yourself.

My name is Marlee Mauvis, and I am a 48-year-old widow and now single mom of two extraordinary boys, ages 16 and 11, as well as a beautiful 22-year-old stepdaughter.

I have been fortunate to experience love, birth and success. I consider my challenges – divorce, disability, failure, death, tragedy and loss – to be events that shaped me. But life's challenges have not and will not defeat me, rather inspire my true purpose – to serve BIG.

I wasn't prepared for the depth of heartache, tragedy and loss that I have experienced over the past 10 years. Most significant has been the death of my husband, Gerard Mauvis – the father and step-father to three beautiful young people. It has given me pause. Significant pause.

At 46, I became a widow and had to learn to re-build my life and re-discover my own voice while taking extraordinary care of children with whom I had been blessed. I had to dig deep to find my faith and purpose again.

To understand my character, strength and determination - my ability to handle all that life has given me, both good and bad, it is important to know what and who shaped me. I was born and raised in Woodstock, New Brunswick, a small town of 5,000 on Canada's east coast.

It's been said that you can take the girl out of the small town, but you can't take the small town out of the girl. True. There's a lot to be said about where we're raised as kids and how that impacts who we become as adults, and the values we carry with us throughout life. This foundation stays with us permanently, and in my case, a big part of my heart is reserved for "home"– home is the heart and soul of the family. That thinking has influenced my roles as a daughter, sister, wife, mother, business professional and friend. These home-town values have grounded me no matter how far I've ventured into the world and allowed me to face life's storms.

In Woodstock, life was simple, and everyone knew your business. Local sports included hunting and fishing, and any drama was played out at the nearest barn dance or high school hockey game. My parents were wonderful, despite their own demons and storms. My mother was a nurse, and from an early age battled mental illness. My father owned the local Esso gas station, and his demon was alcohol, but it was one he confronted and beat – giving up the bottle in his 30's and never touching another drop. My parents proved that devotion to family is everything, loving each other as well as my sister, brother and me unconditionally throughout their challenges.

While my paternal grandmother was a very religious woman and my maternal grandmother was a church-goer, I wasn't brought up in a religious family, but one that was very grounded in love. I did attend Sunday School, but church really wasn't a big part of my life up until about age 42 when we moved to Arizona and really got plugged into a church community. I had faith as a child and I always believed but didn't really practice it. Maybe because I just didn't understand and didn't know where to start, what questions to ask, who to ask, etc. It wasn't until I became an adult, moved here and became involved in a church community, that I was in a better place to ask questions, listen, learn and grow. It became a very real and regular part of our lives. Our community of friends expanded as a result and it really impacted us.

That small town I grew up in was the kind of place where I learned the value of hard work. It was a place where people stayed at one job for 40 years without complaining because they had a responsibility to family and took pride in their job. My parents also reinforced the value of hard work. My mom stayed home raising a family with the odd part-time job, while dad ran the family business – something he did for more than 60 years. Because of their wonderful example, laziness is not in my nature, and you'll often find me not only working hard but fighting for what I believe in both personally and professionally.

I loved playing sports, from basketball and volleyball to soccer and badminton. I was creative in my own way and never afraid to get my hands dirty. Mom would always find me up to something, often mischievous but well-intentioned behavior. Whether it involved a can of paint and paintbrush, a hammer and nails, or rearranging the furniture in the house room-by-room, I was the family's self-proclaimed interior decorator. After all, I was the third and last child – the baby of the family. The free-spirit. And, it's likely that because my older siblings had paved the way with their shenanigans, my parents took an increasingly carefree attitude towards parenting.

Traveling was not common but a luxury, so when I was accepted to Saint Mary's University in Halifax, Nova Scotia, a big city about six hours from home, I was thrilled and anxious to embark on dreams that I didn't imagine possible. I was ready to take on the world and all that life had to offer.

Over the past 25 years, I have leveraged these small-town qualities and experienced a successful career in Telecom, Information Technology, and Hospitality. But my most recent career chapter transpired eight years ago when I took on a role at Franklin Covey as an Account Executive, helping organizations develop their greatest assets: People and Culture.

My work ethic and my values coupled with my family, friends, church community and colleagues have been my support system over the past 18 months. My relationships have been my saving grace.

When you realized single parenting was going to be part of your story, what was your initial response?

When I heard the sickening thud and saw someone in a bright red shirt flying through the air, I knew. I just knew it was my husband. We were going to a high school football game with family and close friends. Gerard dropped off me and our youngest son Will at the stadium entrance and went to park the car. That was the last time I ever saw him. Gerard was crossing the street to meet us but didn't make it. He was struck and killed by a car in an instant and it changed everything.

That was September 30, 2016. I say I knew but I can only say that now as I reflect on that terrible night. I immediately put my arms around Will to block his view, all the while not yet knowing who it was that had been hit. Will heard the noise and asked me what happened. I only said that there had been an accident and a lot of people were trying to help. Gerard had still not arrived, and I was getting worried. I called his cell, but there was no answer and glancing across the street, I saw his car parked. My mind raced. I quickly realized the man with the red shirt who had been struck must have been Gerard. I left Will with a dear friend and ran to the police officer on the scene, asking for confirmation. He showed me Gerard's cellphone case. I was stunned. It was not yet confirmed that my husband had died but my thoughts went wildly there. "Why him, he's so young, he is making an impact, he hasn't finished serving…he has three children including a child with special needs… how am I going to do this on my own? The children, the house, the cars, the maintenance, the mortgage, education, and more. It's just me. One job and one income. God, please help me!"

I sent Will home with our friends. He had no idea what was going on, but he had heard the thud and knew someone needed help.

Friends drove me to the hospital. It was the longest drive of my life and I remember crying out loud, "How far is this hospital?"

Sitting in the waiting room, I knew in my heart-of-hearts that Gerard was gone. I had seen the person in the red shirt fly through the air and couldn't imagine anyone surviving that. As we sat in the waiting room I was already processing the fact that he had died. Finally, the doctor came out. It was written all over her face, and then she spoke the words, "We did everything we could, but we just couldn't save him."

After about an hour, I said, "I have to go home" and left the hospital, arriving home about midnight. I stayed up all night thinking about how and what to tell the kids. How do you tell them their father is dead? I even went online to try to find help with the right words to say. I don't remember if I asked God for help in that instant. I felt betrayed.

The next morning, I told Will about his dad. I referenced the thud he heard and told him "a car hit daddy, and daddy was called to heaven last night and he's not coming home."

Will was initially angry and began processing what I told him. I reassured him that dad was going to keep watching over us, only from heaven and not from here. I had to tell my other son, Harrison, who was away at school, and my step-daughter, Demi, who was halfway around the world. But I made sure they were both with a family member, so they had the support they needed.

And that's when the latest chapter of my story begins, with the sudden and tragic death of a loving husband and father. I hope that revealing my truth, hope and purpose inspires you to find yours too.

I grew up with the mindset – go to school, work hard, get a degree, find a job, get married, have children and live happily ever after. That was the plan. But God had another idea.

They say it takes a village to raise a child. What kind of support systems do you have in place?

Upon hearing about Gerard's untimely death, people traveled from all over the world to help and everyone wanted to be there for us. The funeral was incredible, nearly 1,500 people showed up to the celebration of life for Gerard because people loved him, and everybody loved being with him and those that heard about him wanted to meet him.

From South Africa, and the UK to Canada and the US, I was overwhelmed by the outreach of family, friends, strangers, and many helping hands during the first year without Gerard. It was really about survival. But I surrounded myself with a community that gave me permission to be myself…without judging me

Gerard inspired people and his death made many realize that life is short and that they need to treasure each day. New relationships were formed, as well as job changes and more. People used Gerard's death to reevaluate their own lives and journey. He stimulated many decisions and part of my challenge is to carry on his legacy.

Our faith really came into play in how people responded to Gerard and rallied around us during our time of need. From food and financial donations to funeral arrangements, travel/transportation and more. I simply couldn't handle all of this. The last thing you want to worry about during a time like this is planning meals and how to make the house payment. Other needs were met by so many people and friends.

Everybody Gerard had extended a helping hand to during his lifetime, extended a hand back to us during our time of need and it was amazing to see. It made the first year a lot easier emotionally, spiritually and financially.

Part of the recovery process for Will – who took the loss of his dad the hardest – involves our family's love for football. Sundays were our family days and it was football family day. And "my boys" would sit there together and watch football and just connect as best friends.

Despite being challenged with cerebral palsy, Will took to the field on a Saturday morning just two weeks after losing his dad, to play against another youth football team.

"These boys took to Will, and he took to them like nothing I've never seen," said John Pleskovitch, the President of the Phoenix Storm in an interview for a local TV station that covered the story of one little boy's determination and grit.

Players also wanted to make sure Will got the full experience of playing on the field, which meant putting him in for a chance to play. As the crowd watched and cheered, and with the help of the other team, Will went in and scored a touchdown – in his wheelchair. "He's just always wanted to play football, and he got his chance today," a fellow player said.

Will had a daily route with his dad, which was so cruelly ended. He initially continued to keep up his regular routine, but after six months, Will wanted to quit everything. His grief, expressed in moments of tears and frustration is finally coming out. He talks about his dad and I do something every day to keep Gerard's memory alive.

What has been your biggest challenge and greatest joy while single parenting?

There is no greater joy each day than to see my children smile and laugh. Laughter is the best medicine and drove my motivation. My biggest challenge at first was finding the motivation to get up every day to take care of the kids, getting them to and from school and activities, and helping them with homework, at the same time having no motivation to do anything for myself.

I allowed myself to cry daily, and just forget about life, to the point of losing sight of my diet, exercise and even (at times) sound decision making. I talked about their father every day with the kids like he was present, writing their stories and quotes in a journal. But one thing I never wavered on was my new-found faith, and that God would see me (and us) through this storm.

Having been brought up in a small town, I surrounded myself with a small village that shared in my traditions, values and ideas to not lose sight of where I've been and where I'm also headed. From the school, and community of friends to church and volunteering, we celebrate birthdays, cheer on the local teams and neighborhood kids, host weekly Sunday BBQs, donate our time to serve others, and more.

Work/Life balance. What does that look like for you, and how did you find your rhythm?

Now into my second year as a single-parent – while everyone, outside of our family has settled back into their routines – I find myself focused on finding the balance between a healthy mind, body and spirit so I can be a great mom serving my children and others. Fueling my **MIND** with learning to keep me organized, focused and growing. I recently gleaned three simple questions from Stedman Graham's book *Identity, Your Passport to Success*:
1. What do I Love/What makes me happy?
2. Who do I want to be?
3. What am I doing daily to achieve who I want to be?

These questions have been grounding and provided focus to find balance as a single-parent.

Do you have any single parenting hacks books, or resources other single parents need to know about? And how do you infuse self-care?

In addition to *Identity, Your Passport to Success*, other inspirational works on my bookshelf include:

- *The MacArthur Study Bible ESV*

- *The 7 Habits of Highly Effective People*, by Dr. Stephen R Covey, a business and self-help book presenting an approach to being effective in attaining goals by aligning oneself to principles based on a character ethic that is universal and timeless.

- *The 7 Habits of Happy Kids*, by Sean Covey, a family favorite that has also become great gifts for friends and clients.

- *Love You Forever* by Robert Munsch, a heartfelt story of the evolving relationship between a boy and his mother.

- *Jesus Always* by Sarah Young, devotions that bring joy for each day

- *The 5 Love Languages* by Gary Chapman, a practical approach to understanding yourself and improve all your relationships.

Not to mention fueling my **BODY**, staying hydrated and having water on-hand on hand always, even if it means running to the bathroom often. Getting a good night's sleep, seven hours if possible, so I can focus and be productive.

As for exercise – Ugh!!! Self-care is often a very not-so-beautiful thing. It is enforcing accountability to eating, sleeping, and exercising properly so I can show up and be my best.

Motivated by laughter and smiles, I keep active daily and regularly include a little bit of love and attention to my own body, mind, and soul that I can fit into a short amount of time like playing sports with the kids, biking, and – of course – shopping!

And finally fueling my **SPIRIT** with things I love:

Church – On Sundays, we attend church and host BBQs with friends on Sunday evenings, a tradition Gerard and I started when we moved to Arizona.

Music/Friendships/Family – spending much needed time with my family and friends, whether attending a concert or sharing silly stories of the days/weeks adventures over a fine glass of wine.

Volunteering for MASK, an organization that engages and educates parents, children and the community about the issues facing our youth today and to empower children to make safe, healthy choices.

I am fortunate to work from home where each day I can prepare breakfast and lunch for the kids before seeing them off to school. And, as a bonus, we live close to the school, so I can respond quickly to a fever, appointment or missing homework.

From the moment the alarm rings at 6:30 am, it's GO TIME. We're on a schedule, from breakfast and brushing teeth to clean up and the bus arrival. With Will's special needs, it requires additional time and support for his daily stretching, putting on his leg braces, loading his equipment into the car and more.

Dinner can start at 5 pm, or 6 pm, on the run, or sitting at our kitchen table. Regardless of the time or circumstances, dinner is together, and we reflect on our day. Each family member recounts what made them happy and/or frustrated that day. It's intentional time with one another planned or unplanned that creates memories, and traditions that ground us. And we don't leave the table until everyone is finished.

At bedtime, we say the Lord's Prayer and remember to be thankful for how blessed we are. Although the kids don't always like it and don't want to listen, I keep going, because someday they will do the same for their children. Not to mention, it inspires me and validates where I am on this journey called life.

Building and maintaining a close relationship with my children requires a lot of work, regardless of any situation, so it's important that I:

- Chaperone school field trips.
- Surprise them with special outings to their favorite restaurant, a movie, plays, sporting events, and more.
- Celebrate successes out loud, use special nicknames, and message them daily words of encouragement.

- Do things they don't always expect. Make sure I know what it is that they love to do and do it with them even if it includes video games.
- Hug them often and tell them 'I love you' frequently.
- Get crazy, dance and sing…. life is amazing, so let it shine through.

Because I am on the go, I'm in a constant sweat, so I always keep something healthy in my purse, like nuts, veggies or a protein bar. Not to mention, a great mascara and a nude lip gloss.

Often times you hear that being a single parent means you have to sacrifice your dreams and goals? How have you pursued your dreams and goals in spite of being a single parent?

When it comes to your children, role modeling is everything. Take care of yourself, be dependable, self-reflect and check in with yourself. Be loyal and attentive. Sacrifices are part of life, but it doesn't mean giving up on your dreams and goals. In fact, at 48 years of age, I am fulfilling one of my life's dreams through this book, to be an author.

As I have matured and been through life's experiences, my dreams and goals have become simpler and more intentional. My goal is to help others and serve BIG including advocating for children with special needs and inclusion in the school system, and lobbying government for improved drivers testing policies. Whether that involves founding an organization, changing policies or speaking publicly, God's will guides me.

What advice would you give someone who finds himself or herself in a single parent situation?

The first year without Gerard, I was fortunate to have the support of so many family and friends by my side day in and day out. So, I didn't have a lot of downtime. Grieving took the shape of crying or yelling in the car, in bed or anyplace where no one else was around. What I found most helpful was talking to him out loud whether I was cooking, watching tv, brushing my hair, or talking to the kids at bedtime, and journaling the kid's innocent moments and memories of their dad.

In addition, I was always comforted by signs Gerard was present in the house or wherever we ventured, from butterflies and flickering lights to our favorite songs on the radio. They always presented themselves when I/we needed him, or he needed me/us to know he's watching over us.

If you're going through the loss of a spouse, take the time you need to reflect on your situation, learn from it, and use it for personal growth. Never stop learning because it empowers you.

Ask for help when you need it and accept it when it is offered. People will always ask you how they can help. You are not burdening them; you're only putting more burden on yourself by not accepting their offers of help. The reality is people don't know how you're feeling, and what they should be doing. They've not been in the situation you are. They are here to serve during times of change and need. Let them and tell them what you need.

As we journey on with our new family dynamic, I will continue the old traditions and create new ones. Part of our continuing adventure will be to return every summer to the small town where I grew up and share that with the kids, to continue building those memories and honing those small-town characteristics and values. Parenthood is a blessing. It can be challenging. I will make mistakes, but I will recover... as will my children.

This is my life. I intend to live it to the fullest, serve BIG and in so doing, be a role model and inspiration for my children.

I am, and we are thankful every day for the time we had with my husband, their father. He lived life to the fullest, and he has been called to serve a higher purpose. We are so proud of him, and we know he will forever be our Guardian Angel.

My wish for my children: set goals, follow your dreams and live a purpose-filled life that unleashes your greatest potential. You are capable of anything.

How have you grown personally as a single parent, and what kind of influence do you think that has on your child(ren)?

And, as a single mom, I know that with my faith in God and the support of my friends, faith community and "the kindness of strangers" I too can persevere and move forward. And as you face your dark times and challenges, know that God is with you and will bring into your life those who love you, support you and will encourage you along the journey. Never give up, never stop learning, never stop growing!

Being from a small-town and family routed rich in traditions and ideas, I am determined with GRIT, and blessed by GRACE.

Life is amazing, but it's not fair. We all have a story to tell, and it's our inner character and the choices we make that determine how amazing life can really be – despite the storms.

I'm exactly where I need to be in life and I'm right on track.

God Bless!

MARLEE MAUVIS

For the past 25 years Marlee Mauvis's career has spanned sales, customer service and leadership. In her current position Marlee is fortunate to help organizations develop their ultimate competitive advantage – people. She loves that her role enables her to build capabilities that increases employee engagement and improves business results.

Marlee was born and raised in a small Canadian town where family roots run deep and character is formed. The grit and grace that inspires her personal and professional journey was put to the ultimate test September 2016. Marlee lost her husband suddenly when he was struck by a motorist while crossing the street to attend a high school football game.

At 48, Marlee is a widow and single mother of two extraordinary boys and a beautiful bonus daughter. She considers herself blessed to have experienced love, birth and success and considers her challenges – divorce, disability, failure, death, tragedy and loss – to be events that shaped who she is today. Life's heartaches and challenges have not and will not defeat her. Rather they have and will continue to inspire her to live fully in her true purpose: to serve BIG.

She is passionate about philanthropy, country music, traveling, coaching sales professionals, and making memories with her family.

Connect with Marlee on LinkedIn or Facebook.

YAMACEETA THOMPSON

Tell us a little about yourself.

I am full of hope, I am encouraged to encourage, I am resilient, I am a Mother, a Daughter, a Sister, and a Friend. I am......Yamaceeta Keiosha Thompson. My friends and family call me Yama or Yami. Fun fact: Yamaceeta is of Japanese origin. It is derived from Yamashita, a Japanese surname which means "under the mountain". Yama means mountain as in Fujiyama. Like a mountain, I'm pretty solid. I love people and love helping them discover their gifts and talents. Living out purpose is very important to me.

I've worked in healthcare over 20 years, and am now a Certified Belief Therapist. I help people uncover lies they believe about themselves and other people that are affecting them and hindering progress in areas of their lives. We work to uproot the lies and replace it with truth. The result is quite fruitful.

I absolutely love what I do, but my most rewarding assignment is inside my home. I am the mother to three amazingly gifted and talented young people. Tre' is my 20-year-old prolific singer/songwriter who just completed his A.S. in Commercial Music degree, graduating with Magna Cum Laude honor. Devin is my 15-year-old gentle giant who is a 10th grade German speaking math and science whiz attending a Health Science Academy who aspires to become a Pulmonologist. He's also doing his "thing" with an Alto Sax while leading his school's Black Culture Club as President. Last, but definitely not least, is the caboose, Taiylar Victoria. This 12-year-old princess is our social butterfly and aspiring entrepreneur. She's a leader on her middle school campus, volunteers with a non-profit organization feeding the homeless monthly, and is trying her hand at basketball. Taiylar is also an anointed praise dancer.

I share much about my children because they contribute to who I am today. I thank God for trusting me with their lives, and it is an honor to be their Mommy.

When you realized single parenting was going to be part of your story, what was your initial response?

I welcomed the thought of single parenting. I was never apprehensive about it, because it wasn't scary to me. Although I truly believe in a father and mother led family unit, I moreover believe in a healthy family unit. Once I realized that my children were going to endure much more abuse if I stayed in my marriage "as is", I moved swiftly. I had to protect them. I decided that I'd rather rough it out financially knowing that I could nurture them without a ping pong affect.

They say it takes a village to raise a child. What kind of support systems do you have in place?

My parents, friends, church members, neighbors, and teachers comprise our village. Support systems are great, but they look different in different seasons. When we as single parents understand that, much of our stress may be alleviated. We have to learn to trust God above all else. He's the Chief Strategist and knows exactly what and whom we need and when we need them. Oftentimes, help will come from where we least expect it. All that to say, protect your children, but don't make your village a restricted gated community. Someone may have been sent to help, but they can't if they can't get in.

Work/Life balance. What does that look like for you, and how did you find your rhythm?

Because I'm a dancer, rhythm is very important to me. Fortunately, my current job offers much flexibility to me. I'm able to attend school functions, attend church, and spend quality time with my children. However, it wasn't always that way. As a younger single parent, I worked 2 jobs at the hospital and did a few MLM opportunities. I was always away from home, and one day I just said, "Enough". Little by little, I began taking my time back.

Often times you hear that being a single parent means you have to sacrifice your dreams and goals? How have you pursued your dreams and goals in spite of being a single parent?

There is an element of sacrifice in being a good single parent, but that is not a negative thing. Another thing I have learned is that all things truly work together for our good as The Holy Bible says. I'm a witness! As a single parent, I studied paramedicine to become an EMT. After 1 year, I went on complete my Bachelor degree. Initially, I was going to complete a BSN nursing program I began years before as a traditional college student, but I remembered that during clinicals, I realized that I didn't really want to be a nurse. So, I didn't know what to do with all of those credit hours. I was 13 hours from my BSN. I prayed and prayed. I received some direction and after a little research and consulting with my academic counselor, I found the B.S. in Health Science Management program awarded 30 semester hours for experience in a qualified health field. Well, EMS just happened to fit the bill. Those credit hours catapulted me to a place where I finished my degree program in 1.5 years. I didn't have to retake any classes from the 90's. The university allowed 18 year credits to be used towards my degree. That was God! I furthered my education, and now I'm a certified therapist. I know that I'm where God wants me right now. The beautiful thing about single parenting is that God will interweave your purpose, dreams, and goals right into. I have more dreams and goals, and they will come into fruition at the appointed time!

What has been your biggest challenge and greatest joy while single parenting?

My biggest challenge of single parenting was helping my oldest son, Tre', cope with the divorce and the aftermath. He was very angry. This challenge lasted for many years. As I write, I've been divorced for 13 ½ years. It's been hard forgiving myself for the bad choices I made walking through single parenting that affected him the most. Tre' is doing much better, and I have forgiven myself.

My greatest joy has been getting to know my children as the individuals they are. I love witnessing them blossom and discover what they like and don't like on a grander scale. My greatest joy has been experiencing the ever changing relationship I have with my children. The growing pains and the growing triumphs make it all as unique as a fingerprint, and I'm so glad they belong to me.

Do you have any single parenting hacks, books, or resources other single parents need to know about?

An absolute must resource is Gallup's Strength based parenting. Learning your strengths and learning your child's strengths takes parenting with positive outcomes to a greater level. In any relationship, understanding and accepting an individual's differences is key. The same holds true within the parent-child

dynamic. The Strengths Based Parenting book and assessment tool can take some of the sting out of parenting...period. I wish I had found this resource sooner. I encourage you to look into it today. Here is the website for more information:
http://www.strengthsbasedparenting.com/home.aspx

We live in a busy, rushed culture. How do you infuse self-care into your life?

Hmmmm... Honestly, this one is still a challenge for me. I'm learning to intentionally schedule white space on my calendar. I was consistently over extending myself to the kids, friends, family, and events that I felt I just had to attend. I'm practicing telling myself "No, Yama. You do not need to do that or go there". Setting boundaries for not just others, but even ourselves, puts us steps closer to caring for ourselves...well.

What advice would you give someone who finds themselves in a single parent situation?

Pray. Pray for your children, and teach them how to pray. Remember to breathe, deeply. Remember that your children are blessings and never your enemy. Tough times are temporary. Humility is a virtue, don't be too proud to ask for assistance. Also, listen intently to your children. They need to heard, and sometimes yes sometimes, an answer will come through them. My last piece of advice is to hug your children daily. Nothing compensates for human touch. Take time to hug for at least 20 seconds. Why? Because hugs make a difference. I know because I live it. Real hugs can change your day for the better. Physiologically, 20 seconds hugs are good for you and your child's emotional and physical health. Long enough hugs can increase oxytocin and dopamine which I call the "happy hormones", and lowers the level of cortisol which can lower high blood pressure and aid in better quality sleep. So, stop those quick hugs rushing the kids off to bed. Give them an extended time hug, 20 seconds, it's better than warm milk. Who gives warm milk anymore, anyway?

How have you grown personally as a single parent, and what kind of influence do you think that has on your child(ren)?

Being a single parent grew my faith in God and my integrity. My optimism grew because I really needed to believe for the best no matter what it looked like, sound like, or smelled like. My gumption increased. I believe my personal development has influenced my children positively. I see hope kindling in their eyes in the midst of adversity, when they're down to the wire with a project due or needing a certain grade for that GPA they desire. I see it when their request doesn't get delivered. They have embraced that delayed does not mean denied. Whatever truly is for you, you WILL have it!

YAMACEETA THOMPSON

Servant of God, Intercessor, Mother, Daughter, Friend, Purpose Cultivator, Encourager. Yamaceeta Thompson, a ray of God's "Son"shine, is a native of Westwego, Louisiana currently residing in Plano, Texas. She is the mother of three beautifully gifted children, Tre', Devin, and Taiylar, who enjoys family, music, and theater.

Her formal education and work experience in various facets of healthcare, aligns with her passionate desire and calling to not only assist people I becoming healed spiritually, emotionally, and physically, but to walk beside them. A Certified Belief Therapist, she founded Mountain of Hope Counseling and Coaching Center specializing in helping women move towards recovery, healing, restoration, and purpose. This former EMT's calling to preserve life led to the birthing of Each Beat Counts, a CPR/First Aid Training initiative. Creatively, she is convinced that dancing breathes life...Yamaceeta is the visionary of Silent Anointed Praise Interpretive Dance and Prophetic Movement Ministry. She is also "Miss Inner Beauty Elite- Texas 2015-2017" with a platform of "Pursuing Purpose with Passion" focusing on helping others develop a positive self-image by renewing their minds, igniting hope, and manifesting their life's purpose.

She lives… "Each day is a gift, and I want to share my present with others."

Yamaceeta is a counselor, conference speaker, workshop facilitator, prayer leader, purpose cultivator, and "real talk" panelist who looks forward to connecting with you!

- Email: MountainOfHopeCounseling@gmail.com
- Facebook: The Purpose Cultivator or Yamaceeta Keiosha Thompson
- Instagram: ThePurposeCultivator
- Phone: (469) 795-1293

Favorite Scriptures:

Matthew 6:33 New Living Translation (NLT)
"Seek the Kingdom of God[a] above all else, and live righteously, and he will give you everything you need."

Proverbs 3:5-8 New Living Translation (NLT)
"Trust in the Lord with all your heart; do not depend on your own understanding. Seek his will in all you do, and he will show you which path to take. Don't be impressed with your own wisdom. Instead, fear the Lord and turn away from evil. Then you will have healing for your body and strength for your bones."

FRANCOISE ISAAC

Tell us a little about yourself.

I'm a single adoptive mom of two, and what I know for sure is, there is absolutely no playbook for parenting. You will need to create your own as you go along. I never imagined or planned on being a single parent. God chose this path for me in spite of what I believed.

I've tried to build a village of support by surrounding myself with an army. I'm constantly in search of more soldiers to enhance our family dynamic. When you're a single mom you absolutely need help.

One of my favorite things to do is read, but finding time to do so can be a challenge. There is never enough time in the day for work or mom duty. I try to stay on top of things by keeping track of life's little details in my planner. I'm a "write the vision and make it plain" kind of gal.

Do I have it all together? Definitely not. There are days when I want to pull the covers over my head and ask my Alexa to play sleep sounds. The good news is every day you get to wipe the slate clean and try again.

What keeps me going are three simple words: Faith, Hope and Dream.

When you realized single parenting was going to be part of your story, what was your initial response?

My family has a history of fostering children and my aunt encouraged me to do the same. She fostered children for over 10 years. Each of my grandmothers cared for children by either fostering or adopting them. My own immediate family fostered and adopted my sister when she was about fourteen.

I went through the rigorous licensing and training process for over a year, before the possibility of wanting to do this began to fade. I was getting tired of taking the mandatory training classes, the home inspections and weekly meetings. What was the point in doing all of this, when I never received a call to serve?

I had no intention of adopting but was willing to do temporary fostering and provide respite. I would go to meetings and over hear ladies bragging about how much money they were making. I remember thinking to myself; this is a well-structured side hustle. These women have created a mommy cartel and were running quite a racket.

I was about to contact CPS and tell them to take me off the list when a friend invited me to a cocktail party. As it turned out one of the guests was a psychic medium, who asked me if I me if I had kids. I told him I didn't and in my head I was thinking, "If he's psychic he should know this already. Here we go."

He said I would soon get a girl and a boy. Now I knew he couldn't have been more wrong, because I only signed up for a girl. I told him that couldn't possibly be true because I didn't want a boy. I could flow better with a girl and all my paper work was final. I hoped he would catch the skepticism in my voice, but he didn't.

Next he told me they would be talking to me about a boy and a girl. I asked him, "What if I didn't want a boy and I told them no? My paperwork says a girl! I'm getting a girl!" He said you can't say no because it would change your destiny. "Yeah right!" I told him.

"We'll see." There are a lot of people claiming to be psychic. Heck, I'm a little psychic myself. I put more assurance in the cocktail I was drinking than what he was saying.

A few weeks later I called CPS and told them to take me off the list. I was thinking about moving back to the east coast. The case manager asked me to reconsider my choices and maybe I would get selected to at least provide respite for families that go on vacation. She mentioned I could increase my chances of being able to help someone if I added a boy to the request. She also suggested changing the age range I was willing to work with. It was only for respite and if the call should come in to foster you could always say no. That was something CPS constantly said and reminded me. "You can always say no." I agreed, but in the back of my mind I was still going back home.

Only licensed foster parents can provide respite to foster children. I finally got a call from a woman named Joyce. She was teaching a class for CPS over the weekend and asked if I wouldn't mind watching her two children. It was only for the weekend and I had nothing to do that weekend, so I agreed.

She brought them over during the week, so we could get acquainted. The boy had a friendly personality even though I did have to tell him to stop jumping on my furniture. The little girl was quiet and shy and stayed close to grandma Joyce as they called her. Joyce assured she would warm up to me after getting to know me.

She stayed for a bit, chatting with me a little about their situation. Joyce was a retired police officer from Georgia. She had fostered well over 1200 children in addition to having her own children. She had initially fostered these two for a year before they became eligible for adoption. Well, the adoption didn't work out, which we've learned in training often happens for various reasons. The children were placed back with grandma Joyce. The boy was now 5 and his sister was 2.

I agreed to watch them for the weekend and everything went well. Joyce called me a few weeks later and said she was tired and just needed a break. She asked if I could watch the kids again and I agreed. This time she chatted a little more about their situation.

The little girl suffered from a traumatic brain injury (TBI) sometimes referred to as "shaken baby syndrome". This resulted from blunt force trauma to the brain causing a skull fracture at 8 weeks. A full body scan revealed over 100 broken bones including ribs that were on the mend and both broken ankles appeared to be healing at the time of intake. The result of her injuries caused left side weakness with the inability to fully use her left hand. She also suffered from seizures which is typical post brain surgery. Most children with these injuries do not survive. The miracle was she did and her brain remapped itself.

The boy showed no recent outward evidence of abuse. CPS could not get a full body scan to determine any prior injuries. However, scars from whip marks were evident on the backs of his legs. At the time of the incident he was 3 years old and did not speak. Initially, CPS believed this was because a second language was spoken in the home.

Evidence later proved that not to be the case. He did not speak because he was not spoken to. He was drugged most of the time to stay asleep, while his parents did drugs and worked most of the days and nights. Grandma Joyce was proactive about putting him in speech therapy and by age 5 he was speaking well and coherently.

What I didn't realize at the time, is Joyce was also checking me out. You see, she was facing a dilemma and had a small window of time to take action. The family that initially wanted to adopt the kids had decided they only wanted to adopt the little girl and not the boy. Once a sibling group is placed in your home and deemed as having a sibling bond they cannot be separated. If the family decides they want to do this, all children are immediately taken from the home and returned to CPS custody.

Their current foster family had taken this matter to court and said a barrage of horrific things about the young man. The judge mandated if there was no expressed interest in adopting the children by a certain time, he would split them up. The family would be free to adopt the girl and the boy would return to foster care. This posed an even bigger problem. Because he was an African American boy age 5, statistics indicated he would be harder to place or adopt. Eventually he could end up in a group home. Even I knew that.

I was not okay with another black family being split up. That enraged me more than anything. There is no way that family could possibly understand what that meant. I was not okay after meeting these children with allowing them to be thrown out in the world like fishing nets hoping somebody would catch them. I was not okay knowing the boy showed no evidence of the nonsense they said on paper ending up in a group home. I thought about the women in those meetings. These kids could get thrown into their money pit. I thought about what that psychic told me and said a curse word under my breath.

Many people were approached to take on the children, but out of 26 candidates including their own family members none of them were suitable. They either did not pass the drug tests, financial, or psychological requirements. Grandma Joyce was on a mission to find the right family for them and she picked me. CPS picked me.

I consulted with my friends and they all told me I should under no circumstance do this. I had no idea what I was getting into. Plus, those kids could be messed up. I conferred with family. Some of which, said no, but my mom said she felt like I could do it. I discussed the pros and cons with my online social media friends and they told me it was a decision I had to make on my own.

I have three character flaws that I am willing to admit. The first being I am too smart for my own good. The second one is that I do what I want. The third one is once you tell me no, it's like activating the launch sequence.

If God came down here right now and told me He put those two children in my path to help, what would be a good enough reason to tell Him why I had chosen not to? How exactly would I account for my lack of action? My conversation with God went something like this:

Me: It would be too hard?
God: Being a Christian is hard.
Me: I wanted to move back home.
God: You still can move back. I brought you here. I can send you back.
Me: I don't have enough money.
God: I always provide. Even when you don't have money, you know you have money.

Me: I'm not married. They need a mother and father.
God: I am their father.

I couldn't think of one thing convincing enough to tell God. On January 18, 2008 I said yes. I cried the first day I got them right there at the dinner table. My life as I had known it, was gone. I mourned the loss of me until my son asked, "Are you not well? Does your tummy hurt?" I had to pull it together and figure out a way to balance the old me with the new me. I had to create a new normal. My daughter touched my arm while drinking her bottle and my son said. "That means she likes you."

They say it takes a village to raise a child. What kind of support systems do you have in place?

We have a therapist that we see biweekly and a psychiatrist that we see monthly. My daughter has annual visits to the neurologist as a result of her TBI. My children's entire medical team understands and supports me. They absolutely try to make things better for us and I appreciate that. After adoption you are on your own to figure everything out.

My best friends live in various parts of the country and they keep me sane. Most of which, I've known since my childhood. I honestly could not make it emotionally and physically without them. I often brag that I have the best friends in the world and I really do. There have been times where I just couldn't go any further. I mean I have been physically worn down with dark circles under my eyes and they have taken over. They are my daily dose of therapy.

Make sure you stay in constant contact with your children's teachers. I believe my role is to support them with helping my children learn. My daughter has many challenges and it's important to work as a team, if there is ever going to be any hope for her to become a functional part of society. My challenge reminds me of the lyrics to a Billie Holiday song that says, "The difficult I'll do right now. The impossible will take a little while."

My son for the most part is a good student, but he can't be left to his own devices. I have to step in from time to time and get him back on track. He has difficulty with staying focused and his short term memory is not very good. He's very much into technology. He goes to a high school that is STEAM based and project focused. STEAM is an educational approach that covers Science, Technology, Engineering, the Arts and Mathematics.

I think it's important for children to connect socially and participate in organizations that support how I'm trying to raise them. Both of my children participate in enrichment programs like Big Brother's Big Sisters and programs sponsored by The North Dallas Chapter of Delta Sigma Theta. Their agenda is designed to prepare them for the future by building their self-esteem and providing them with the tools they need to succeed. They touch on various themes some of which include leadership, STEAM, etiquette, community service, financial wellbeing and building strong character.

I also share job postings, recipes, crafts, parenting tips and anything that might be of interest to single parents on a Facebook page I manage called, Parenting Alone Resource Group. There are a ton of resources available and I'm happy to share what I know and what I have.

Lastly, I am a member of The Gifts for Moms Project and serve on their advisory board. The Gifts for Moms Project provides peer-to-peer support and is a non-profit organization. We help each other by sharing knowledge and resources. Sometimes that comes in the form of information, money, furniture, clothing and education.

I naturally gravitated toward this group because it is the embodiment of the Ubuntu philosophy I subscribe to. Ubuntu means, I am because we are. If I have, you have. You do what you do best and share it with your village. At my grandma Payne's funeral, her final request was that we always remember to take care of the family. This is how I honor her and the village I serve.

Work/Life balance. What does that look like for you, and how did you find your rhythm?

I am a self-professed workaholic. I deal with a lot of questions and problems all day and working with numbers can become pretty intense. Some days it may take you a few hours to find that missing penny. When I'm in a zone and deep in concentration, I don't like to be disturbed. If left to my own devices I would work for at least 12 hours a day. I like to under promise and over deliver. In order to do that, you have to be prepared.

A work/life balance for me means all systems are a go at work and home. I've always been blessed with an incredible staff that knows what they are supposed to do and how to do it. Creating an environment that fosters collaboration and teamwork helps a lot. I need to know when I'm not in the office my team can maintain the integrity of the workload and resolve problems with diplomacy. I haven't had a team yet that didn't rise to this occasion.

Once the kids arrived, I had to slow everything way down and figure out some sort of balancing system. During the school year I don't spend my time frivolously. There is too much going on between dinner, homework and projects. Visiting friends, sitting around chit chatting is my least favorite thing to do now. I'm always thinking about what I could be doing instead.

I make check lists at home and work daily. I constantly carry a calendar with me to keep track of important work dates and doctor appointments. I realize there is an app for that, but I actually hate electronic devices and telephones. It's just another thing we have become slaves to. Putting pen to paper and crossing things off feels more empowering and accomplished to me.

I try to prepare as much as possible for tomorrow. I give myself permission to not be perfect even though it kills me. Inevitably there will be something that puts a monkey wrench in your entire program. Compartmentalize what you need to and keep it moving. As a caregiver, I need to take care of myself in order to take care of my children. My job as their mom is to keep them safe and make them feel safe. Children in foster care system tend to be those in greatest need and have experienced Post Traumatic Shock Disorder (PTSD). There will be good days and bad days. The goal is to create more good days through love, security and caring.

Often times you hear that being a single parent means you have to sacrifice your dreams and goals? How have you pursued your dreams and goals in spite of being a single parent?

I have never been able to shake the east coast determination in me no matter where I've lived. That means, I do what I want even if I have to get the rules changed. If I want something I go get it. It starts with writing my vision down. I even have a bulletin board with a wish list of initiatives I want to achieve at work. As they become a reality, I erase them from the board.

I have made a lot of sacrifices since becoming a single mom. I don't travel nearly as much as I used to because it's so expensive for all of us. Being a single mom you learn to become more resourceful than you ever knew you could be. There's nothing more satisfying than working deals when you are stone cold broke and leaving the store with a full bounty.

This year I wanted to really challenge myself by doing something that made me feel a little uncomfortable. This writing project was one of them. I don't consider myself a writer although people most often ask me to help them with writing assignments. When you are asked to embark upon something, you either jump right in or wonder what if. I always like to throw the dice one more time. I've just got to give it a shot.

What has been your biggest challenge and greatest joy while single parenting?

The biggest challenge is dealing with the after effects of my daughter's traumatic brain injury and not knowing what resources are available to help us. Initially, she was like any other child. However, as time went on we realized her coping mechanism was not functioning at age capacity. Doctors and therapists believe she can be trained to overcome how she copes with situations, but it will take time.

She has gone through a barrage of tests, year over year. Traumatic brain injuries can take many forms and each person's reaction is different. Most children with her injuries don't even survive. Because she is a medically complex patient, medications may not work as they are designed. She is on a lot of medication to control seizures, ADHD, as well as behavior. Each day we have little breakdowns or episodes of childlike defiance and by Sunday I am truly spent.

There are limited resources for children with TBI's. The assumption is most people sustain traumatic brain injuries as adults. Who would expect someone to intentionally do this to a child? Besides which, most children with TBI's at that early age die. As a result of that assumption there are tons of resources for adults with TBI's. We will have lots of help by the time she reaches adulthood. In the meantime and in between time, I'm the one left having to tough this out, relying on the medical professionals and my village until then.

The greatest joy by far is how funny they are. You can't let them know this of course, but their take on the world is sometimes hysterical. Seeing them developing and changing is funny too. They always think they are telling you something new. I think I was far more prepared for the world at their age, but it was a different time.

There is one thing that seems to be universal between our two worlds and that is music. I love influencing them with my music. My kids know who Prince is and after his death my daughter refused to do any school work until the teacher played Purple Rain. She obliged of course, in order to avoid a tantrum.

My son picks up on original songs that are later sampled in the music he listens to. For example, Ray Charles' "I got a woman way across town" and Kanye West's "God Digger." Because he is musically inclined he likes to listen to both versions. He's a deep thinker so Marvin Gaye's "Trouble Man" album really appeals to him especially after it was mentioned in a Marvel movie.

It's funny to hear them singing Nancy Wilson's "How Glad I Am", in the car or my daughter signing her heart out to Aretha Franklin's "Natural Woman". If she only knew what she was singing? This past Christmas we were in the car and I had a slight headache. I was about to put a New Edition CD on, but I warned them if anybody sang they wouldn't get anything for Christmas.

They sat quietly for about a minute. The suspense was killing them. Suddenly, my son had an epiphany. He shouted, "Hey you said we weren't getting anything for Christmas anyway!" That was the queue they needed and the next thing I heard at the top of their lungs was, *"Candy girl you are my world. You look so sweet. You're a special treat."* I had to pull the car over because I was laughing so hard.

Accepting your kids as they are helps a lot, but you really need to be honest with yourself about their limitations. Sometimes you have to surrender to the inevitable and stick and move around your circumstance. Your kid is not going to be a rocket scientist. Okay? Now think about what they are going to be and develop them as best you can in that regard.

Do you have any single parenting hacks, books, or resources other single parents need to know about?

As a single parent I recommend that you:

1. Join or create a support group.

2. Be as prepared and organized as you can be. Plan for the unexpected and if that fails pick and choose what you allow to make you crazy. You can't fall apart over everything.

3. Practice Ubuntu. I am because we are. Build your village.

4. Make time to take care of yourself. Remember your inflight safety instructions. *"If you are traveling with a child or someone who requires assistance, secure your mask on first, and then assist the other person."*

5. Keep a piggy bank in the kitchen, laundry room, bedrooms, car and at work. When you have change, bank it. If you ever find yourself strapped for cash this can at least get you through a tiny rough patch.

6. When you take the children shopping, tell them if it is a "Looking Day" or "Buying Day". If it's a Looking Day they cannot ask for ANYTHING. If it's a Buying Day, they are able to ask for ONE THING. This cuts down on tantrums in the store, can I have and teaches delayed gratification of a want.

7. Sell your children's gently used clothing to a local resale store. What doesn't get purchased donate to charity and save the receipt for your tax deductions.

8. Sign your children up for organizations that help support your goals for them. A lot of organizations are free and this

gives you time to regenerate as well. It may be the only chance you get to hide those holiday gifts.

9. Link up with a Social Service organization that has a Case Manager that can help you with resources that meet your particular need.

10. Don't be afraid to ask for help. Remember, you have not for you ask not. James 4:2

We live in a busy, rushed culture. How do you infuse self-care into your life?

I am an active member of the Savvy Sistah's book club, going on 14 years now. I have always loved to read. When I was a commuter in NYC, I would read up to five books a week. I miss that. We meet monthly and I absolutely love this diverse group of ladies. I find their conversations both fascinating and stimulating. If I can't make my monthly book club meetings, I am beyond disappointed. It's an absolute necessity.

These women are mothers, grandmothers, wives, nurses, teachers, engineers, motor cycle riding, fast car driving, comedic (not on purpose), and likeminded individuals. We rarely agree to disagree which is why the group has existed since 2002. Not only do we discuss the book of the month, but we talk about politics, entertainment and current affairs. They are a powerhouse of information for me and help restore my rhythm.

I also made a pledge on my vision board to remember to take time for me. This year I've committed to getting a monthly massage.

I have an annual arrangement with a local spa for as little as $50.00 a month. Everyone should allow themselves this one indulgence.

I also get a manicure and pedicure every two weeks. I used to get this done every week before having kids. I take my losses and celebrate the small victories. Sometimes I even get false eyelashes. Wink.

What advice would you give someone who finds themselves in a single parent situation?

First of all, exhale! If you are in a position to do so, remember you can always say no. In fact, you will have to learn how to say no more often. You will no longer be able to do some of the things you used to do when it was just you. Attempts to be the same will become futile.

You are kidding yourself if you think your house will stay in order at all times. I remember a social worker telling me how nice and clean my house was. She said she wanted to come back in a few years to see how it looked. She jinxed me which made me add a housekeeper to my vision board. I am entirely too tired to keep up with everything. I hate doing laundry and putting it away. I still enjoy cooking, but sometimes I wish I didn't have to do it as often. Kids can't skip meals or eat a bowl of cereal as you might like to do.

Build your army of people and network to find out about more resources. Build your army with friends, church members, teachers, doctors and family. Don't be afraid to ask stupid questions. Those are often the ones that get you the best answers. You never know who may know something of value to you. When I'm at my single mom's support meetings I always leave armed with useful information.

Practice Ubuntu. I am because we are. Ask for help and remember it's okay to be imperfect. You are not superwoman and you may never be. When you ask for help talk about what your most basic need is right now. Goals start as lists. Make a list of things you absolutely need and things you want. Turn them in to mini-tasks and eventually you will accomplish them.

Prepare in advance as much as possible. That includes meals, lunches and what we are wearing tomorrow. Keep a calendar of important dates and appointments. Delegate age appropriate chores. As they get older this is a big help.

Sign your children up for programs that support how you want to raise them. I sign up for everything that comes my way. You have a responsibility to expose them to every opportunity possible. They become a better global citizen and gives you time to regenerate. They need to have other forms of motivation that don't center on electronic gadgets.

Finally, make time for yourself. Do grown up things. Don't put your daughter's barrettes in your hair. If you do this, you are truly gone. This indicates a person that is child consumed. You need to find balance in your life. Pamper yourself and allow for a few small things like pedicures, candles, shower gel and a night out.

How have you grown personally as a single parent, and what kind of influence do you think that has on your child(ren)?

I have more strength than I ever knew existed. My patience may be thin, but it's held up a lot longer than most of my friends thought it would. I think this new found strength comes from living in your reality. It is what is and there is no point or value in pretending that it's not. You can't get anything accomplished if you are in denial. It's a disservice to yourself and eventually to your child.

If you know your child has special needs address it now. Otherwise, you will end up with an inept adult making their own decisions. You find yourself in a power struggle about their rights and resources. Face the reality and start planning now.

I hope my children learn from my compassion for others. In addition to taking on my children, I have taken in friends and their children from time to time. I hope my children grow up knowing instinctively that sometimes people need help. If you are in a position to help them, do it. It is a blessing to be able to help someone else.

I have always been good at brainstorming. That is really my passion. The one thing I am really good at. If I could make a living by brainstorming, I certainly would. I have become the most resourceful person I know and I enjoy sharing that information.

If I give ideas and resources and you don't follow through that really pops my balloon. I tend to worry about your situation more than you do. When you lose steam, I have to remind myself to lose steam too. Although I get compassion fatigue it doesn't deter me from continuing to help others. I hope my children know that when we fall down, we get right back up.

My son's biggest fear is that something will happen to me and he will become responsible for his sister. He is afraid of having to give up his dreams. I now have a life insurance policy and advanced directive. My children came from foster care. The last thing they need to worry about is if they have to go back there. I've made provisions to insure their future.

Our family song is Tomorrow (A Better You, A Better Me) by Quincy Jones featuring Tevin Campbell. I've instructed my children, when I close my eyes for the last time and this voice can no longer soothe, warn or scold, listen to this song. It holds my instructions and directive on how they should live their life. I can't let anything stand in the way of their hopes and dreams. I am responsible for them from start to finish.

FRANCOISE ISAAC

Francoise was born and raised in New Jersey and graduated from Kimball Union Academy in Meriden, New Hampshire. She went on to earn a B.A. in Sociology from Duquesne University in Pittsburgh, Pennsylvania. She is a member of the National Association of Professional Women and Serves on the advisory Board of The Gifts for Moms Project as Vice President.

Francoise moved to Texas in 2004 after enjoying a fourteen-year career as a Credit Manager for MTV Networks in New York. Once she migrated to Dallas, she worked as the Assistant Business Manager for Radio One in Dallas and Avnet, Inc., one of the world's largest distributors of electronic components as Manager of Financial Operations.

Fran's passion for improving the lives of children led to her to fostering two siblings, and subsequently adopting them on National Adoption Day in 2009. She finds life as a single parent both challenging and rewarding. She recognized early in the experience that there is no playbook on how to be a parent. As she puts it:

"You really need to be armed with great information and a variety of resources. I try to share as much information as I can. As I learn new things, I share them. I would love to launch a blog that single parents could look to for really great resources. That is on my bucket list."

In her spare time, Fran is an avid reader and a faithful (13 year) veteran of the Savvy Sisters Book Club. She enjoys playing Bunco, helping her children with school projects, and traveling. She subscribes to, and practices the Southern African philosophy of Ubuntu, which means "I am, because we are. Alone we are nothing, but together we can accomplish great things."

CAROLYN DAVID-GRAVES

When you realized single parenting was going to be part of your story, what was your initial response.

The reality of being a single parent was extremely devastating for me. I dreaded becoming a single parent more than the death of my marriage. I was very ashamed and felt I was no longer worthy of being a member of my Antiguan family. Throughout life, I have experienced and known a lot of wonderful single parents however, it was not part of my frame of reference. So, the reality of single parenting was almost unfathomable for me.

Growing up, most of my family and friends were from two-parent homes. Husband and wives stayed married until one of them died. I grew up with both parents at home so, I never imagined a day would come where I would be a single mother. My biological parents, Charles and Idabelle David, were 7 months away from celebrating their 50th wedding anniversary, when my Dad passed away from cancer. His loss was extremely devastating to me because they were never not together.

As my reality of single parenting became clearer, I realized that though married, I was always a single parent! My then husband and I worked different schedules – he worked nights, I worked days. This left the brunt of caring for the children to me. The day he left I felt lost, but the children jolted me back to reality and somewhere deep down inside, I believe through divine intervention and with the help of wonderful friends and family, I was able to adjust to being a single parent. One of the most freeing things that happened was when my mom looked me deep in the eye and said, *"Carolyn, you are a wonderful mother! Whether single or alone, you are raising wonderful children. I am very proud of you and the woman you have become. You have not brought any shame to your father or me. Walk with your head up and serve God!"*

As a Christ follower, I truly believe it is not in God's design for anyone to parent alone. However, I truly understand the dynamics of and reasons for single parenting. The stigma and shame I felt because of my cultural heritage were replaced with a passion to honor God's word in raising my children as expressed in Proverbs 22:6, *"Train up a child in the way he should go, and when he is old he will not depart from it."* With God as my guide, I endeavor to raise my children with the 5-C's: Confident, Christian, Citizens, Contributing to their Community and the world! While this is my prayer and focus, I cannot fully claim to have developed it, a workshop presenter in Louisville, Kentucky shared it with me.

They say it takes a village to raise a child. What kind of support systems do you have in place?

This is not just a saying but one that is true in my sphere of childrearing. I believe we are extensions of our families and we are more secure when we have a support system; a place of identity. I was born into a four-generational family. Words almost fail to describe the security I felt as a member of that family. I was not only my parent's child but the child of whose company I was in at any given time. Love, support, guidance and correction came from family members and fellow villagers alike. Church was the nucleus of our community bringing all the family and community ties together.

My children and I have many friends and family members who support us. We have always lived in areas away from biological family, so we found support at church. We found friends who not only support us but with whom we can be totally open and honest. Friends who provide gentle correction and rebuke when needed. We would not have made it without the wonderful support of so many who have poured into our lives. We have friends and church families we can turn to at any time.

As I am writing this section, I cannot help but pause to acknowledge the wonderful pastors and congregations of the following churches: St. Paul's Anglican, Faith Wesleyan Holiness, Akron Alliance Fellowship, First Virginia Avenue Missionary Baptist, Graceland Baptist and Hunters Glen Baptist. Without you we would fit every bad stereotype.

Work/Life balance. What does that look like for you, and how did you find your rhythm?

The concept of work/life balance is one that is talked about in many forums. I often hear about being on an airplane and instructed to put on my mask first. I see a lot of wisdom in doing so. However, it is very hard for me to not only conceptualize this thought but put it into practice. To me, and based on how I was raised, parents care for their children and in turn the children care for their parents. My formative years in Antigua shaped that thinking and it is very hard to accept the mindset that a work/life balance is necessary to function. I remember my mom taking morning breaks with several of her close friends to listen to radio-broadcasted soap operas; *Portia Faces Life* is one that comes to mind. At other times, they would take time to congregate in a pasture or on the church grounds to share life stories and give advice while we, their children, ran and played. My mom would also take time to read. To those women and me, this was work-life balance.

Looking at my life, I have very little breaks from my children. However, there are times I can pull away to socialize with friends, attend a seminar, go to the nail or hair salon or get a massage. When I was younger, I travelled extensively and did many things some would only dream of, because; I knew the day I became a wife and mom, my life would be dedicated to being her. One may look at my life and consider it boring. I consider myself blessed to be able to invest in raising my children to realize the 5Cs, mentioned earlier.

As I age, I realize that it's ok to pull away from the noise of life and retreat to home and the sanctuary of God's Word. There is so much balance there!

Often you hear that being a single parent means you must sacrifice your dreams and goals? How have you pursued your dreams and goals despite being a single parent?

As a single mom, I have had to put my dreams and goals; on hold for my children. Over the last few years, my family has been challenged in many ways. We went through a hostile divorce, I became unemployed, my daughter developed kidney failure from strep throat and we were recently told she would require a transplant. We moved away from our sanctuary of friends and family to Texas where we knew no one – it was the only place I was able to find a job. We had to adjust to that transition and still are. My mom passed away approximately 1 month later; after that, my eldest son went off to college and due to finances, we had to move 6 times since relocating to Texas. Life has not been easy! Every personal dream and goal had to take a backseat to the cascade of difficult life situations we had to endure. The hardest part was the children looked to me so, I had to lead and decide while feeling like I was falling apart.

As we faced and endured each struggle, I am fully reminded of how the Lord extends grace and mercy during our times of need. According to Proverbs 16:9, *"A man's heart plans his way, But the Lord directs his steps."* Very often our goals and dreams are born out of feelings, societal notions, promptings by others or a desire to be like someone. We don't usually stop to consider God's plan for our lives and His timing. We may be destined to achieve the goals and dreams we set for ourselves but sometimes God wants us to be still and know that He has a better plan for our lives.

I've always wanted to become either an attorney, physician or psychologist. Today, I am neither. However, my life is fulfilled in ways that if I never achieve any of those goals, I wouldn't miss anything. My perspective has changed, and I realized that through single parenthood the Lord is allowing me to become more of who He created me to be and to live out all three professions as I raise my children. In their disputes, I am an attorney. When they are sick, I am their physician. When they are hurting emotionally, I am their psychologist. Perhaps one day soon, I will be able to pursue one of those professions.

At this phase of my life, I truly believe the Lord is allowing our family to be a testimony to others as we endure the challenges we currently face. The bible says that no one can see God and live, so we are His representatives here on earth being powerful testimonies of encouragement and faith to others who may be doubting His existence. I have chosen to align my goals and dreams with His plans for me. It is in that place of surrender where my true purpose will become evident and I will realize that the plans He has for me are more than I could ever dream. Right now, this is the perfect place for me!

What has been your biggest challenge and greatest joy while single parenting?

Since becoming a single parent, my greatest challenge has been to deal with all the difficult life situations and choosing to surrender it all to the Lord without giving in to my natural tendencies, finding a quick replacement husband or using drugs or alcohol to numb the pain.

When others hear our story and the difficulties we have endured as a family, they often ask, "How have you not lost your mind? Others would remark, "If it were me, I don't know if I would survive." Believe me, there are many times I wanted to run away and give up! There are many times, I wanted to go to the bar and "drown my sorrows" Unfortunately, the sorrows resurrect when you get sober!

On this journey, I have realized that God is faithful despite what is going on in my life. The following verses have encouraged and strengthened me when I feel like giving up:

- **John 14:18** - "I will not leave you orphans; I will come to you."
- **Genesis 28:15** - "Behold, I am with you and will keep you wherever you go, and will bring you back to this land; for I will not leave you until I have done what I have spoken to you."
- **Jeremiah 29:11** - For I know the thoughts that I think toward you, says the Lord, thoughts of peace and not of evil, to give you a future and a hope.

- **Joshua 1:9** - Have I not commanded you? Be strong and of good courage; do not be afraid, nor be dismayed, for the Lord your God is with you wherever you go."
- **Hebrews 12:4-11** - In your struggle against sin you have not yet resisted to the point of shedding your blood.

Through faith in His word and the support of my church and biological families and many friends, we have been rebuilding our life. When my ex-husband left, he literally took everything! Our home and bank accounts were emptied, utilities were turned off in addition to leaving a large debt.

Since becoming a single parent, I can joyfully say that through God's grace, I was able to pay off the debt, save and since then sell our home, relocate to a new state, saw my eldest graduate high school and is now a sophomore in college and is making wise choices. While writing, my oldest said to me, "*Mom, I am so proud of you! You are moving out of the funk you were in and moving towards improving yourself and making a better life for us.*" What joy!

Do you have any single parenting hacks, books, or resources other single parents need to know about?

The Internet [Pinterest, Facebook, Google, etc.] is replete with resources for single parents. Over the years, these two websites have been my go-tos for resources for any area of parenting and a mother's life: Focus On the Family: https://www.focusonthefamily.com/ and WorkingMom.com: http://www.workingmom.com/ .

Tips:
- Read through the book of Psalms and Proverbs and Ecclesiastes 12 with your children. They are filled with wise sayings and instructions for life. This could be done each day and will generate a lot of family discussion while teaching you and your children how to honor the Lord, love, cherish and value self and others.
- Cook meals with your children on the weekend. This reduces the burden of cooking a meal each day and helps reduce spending on fast food and other unhealthy options. Besides it's a great family activity.
- Reserve times for home work, rest and family togetherness each week. In our family, we try to get all work done by Thursday. Friday is family night and Saturday Sabbath or rest day.
- Involve children in decisions that affect the family. It helps them own and invest in maintaining the household and respecting the budget.
- Teach children to clean and help around the house. If they can sit around playing electronic games and being on social media, they can operate any household appliance.
- Take children to the local library and let them borrow books. Have them write book reports or give summaries during family night. This will help them develop and practice skills that will be useful throughout their lives.
- Be a giver and encourage children to do so. This will help them develop compassion and empathy and help them become less selfish.
- Teach children your family history so they have a foundation and a place of origin which will help boost their self-confidence and sense of belonging.

- Teach children how to respect their elders and those in authority; to develop a sense of national pride and patriotism.
- Teach them to respect God's creation and to value the earth and the privilege to live in it.
- Most important model a God faring life, demonstrate care for others and live with honesty, trust and integrity. With children, more is caught than taught!

We live in a busy, rushed culture. How do you infuse self-care into your life?

Like work/life balance, I struggle in this area. I often forego caring for myself to do or be something for my children. I believe there is no honorable position on earth than being a parent and shaping the next generation. One of the things I always try doing is using the drive to and from work or whenever I am alone to pray and de-stress. I also try to limit social media and telephone conversations with a cut-off time of 10:00pm. I am not always successful but, I do try!

At various times throughout my single-parent journey, I would take a few hours to go to the beauty and nail salon or to get a massage. This is often sporadic as finances are tight and other things take priority. These I often do myself mostly after the children have gone to bed, early in the morning or after most of the chores are completed.

I like singing, so going to church on Wednesdays for choir practice and doing daily devotions in the morning and night are ways I interject self-care into my life. I sing and pray throughout the day for self-encouragement. Sometimes, taking a warm bath or shower and applying perfume or scented oils before going to bed is one of the most refreshing things I do for myself. I also visit the chiropractor each week.

What advice would you give someone who find themselves in a single parent situation?

The first thing I would tell a new single parent is accept your situation! It may not be what you planned but, it is what it is. Children did not ask to be born. They are your responsibility. Prioritize your life so you can raise them to become productive and successful adults.

Enlist the help of those around. It is the hardest job you will ever do. You cannot do it alone. If you do not have a support group find or form one. Many churches have groups in which you and your children can participate. It is a way to build community while giving you time to be with other adults and your children with their peers.

Develop a routine and try to stick to it. It is easy to get tired and frustrated which often leads to being overly strict or too permissive. This confuses children and they will always try to push you in ways to get what they want and end up without proper discipline or instruction. Very often this creates more frustration and can lead to unintended consequences.

Find time to care for yourself. If it is singing, exercising, praying or just watching television, whatever that looks like for you, take the time to do it. You may not believe in the God of the Bible like I do; however, it is important to take time to nourish your soul through prayer, meditation, petitions, song or whichever way works best for you; even if it means throwing your apron over your head like the mother of John and Charles Wesley.

Finally, everyone has advice about how you should raise your children and what you are not doing right. Find someone who is doing it right and ask them to mentor you. Throughout my life I have had many mentors. I will be forever grateful to my biological parents Charles and Idabelle David, my spiritual parents Carlston and Constance Christie, Gus and Elaine Brown, Robert and Helen Wright and Sharon and Terry Tanner. They have all taught me how to live a life of devotion to the Lord, care for others and live a life of integrity. To the woman who taught me how to be an effective single parent and my greatest cheerleader, Deitra Byrd-Rogers, I cannot thank the Lord enough for your love and instruction throughout the years and for adopting me as your child!

Being blessed with those loving men and women who mentored me through various life stages is the reason, I am enduring as a single parent. Finding a mentor and cheerleader is one of the greatest assets you can have as a single parent. Besides, they become bonus aunts, uncles and grandparents for your children.

How have you grown personally as a single parent, and what kind of influence do you think that has on your children.

Last December, my children and I sat down for a family meeting to plan for the coming year, 2018. I was expecting them to make suggestions about travel and various activities they wanted to participate in and birthday parties they wanted to have. Instead, the children told me they appreciated me as a mom, but I needed to get a life for myself. They shared how hard I work, that I am always with them, but they are growing up and will soon be gone. They advised me to start pursuing my dreams and making new friends. They even told me I needed a boyfriend! Boy, was I shocked!

I vowed then to start pursuing some of the things that would recapture the essence of who I am. Since January, I have started exercising. I also started working part-time with 5Rings Financial, a financial services company that hosts free workshops to teach the principles of money and how to make decisions that will provide financial security and change the trajectory for families. This is an awesome networking opportunity that not only helps me make a difference in the lives of others; it also gives me the satisfaction of sowing into families in one of the most important ways for generations.

Looking back over the last 5 years, I have grown in ways I did not realize. I am more self-less. I am learning how not to take life, others and myself too seriously. I am not as selfish as I was. I am more willing to stand up for what I believe. I am committed to not compromising my walk as a Christ Follower or being desperate for the company of others even when they don't believe or respect my values.

My spiritual Dad, Carlston Christie, would often say to me, "The unexamined life is not worth living." Now, I take the time to examine how I am living. I am in the process of re-branding me by developing my Why; my purpose for getting up in the morning and the passion that drives me. I am a work in progress and it has empowered my children to confront me to becoming a better me. By God's grace, I will!

CAROLYN DAVID-GRAVES

Having endured so much, it's almost difficult to describe myself in a concise way that makes sense. However, before becoming a single parent, I would describe myself as being semi-fulfilled and living the American dream. Today, I realize that I am a more experienced and bigger version of the little girl who delighted in skipping to her grandmother's house with goodies in a hand-basket, ensuring everyone was cared for and one who waited excitedly for my Dad to come home and was overcome with inexplicable emotion just at the sight of him.

I grew up in a small fishing village on the South East side of Antigua in the Caribbean. My father was a seasonal fisherman and chef, my mother was a housewife and I had 10 brothers and sisters. Life in my little village could be regarded as being poor but, we did not know it! When we were not in school or church, we would be spending time with cousins too numerous to mention, sitting at the feet of an elder family member listening to the best stories, or exploring our playground which stretched from the ocean to the hills that served as a backdrop for our village. Back then, life was almost perfect!

As I graduated high school and started working, I decided to leave Antigua to attend university. My educational journey led me to the Virgin Islands then to various states in the United States. Each leg of the journey was interspersed with wonderful family and friends who sowed into my life in many ways; helping me become the woman I am now.

Today, I am a single mother of three beautiful children, Joshua, LeMae and Leon. Outside of my relationship with the Lord, they are who I live for. I enjoy spending time with them, watching them grow and surprise me with their uniqueness. They are the joys of my life; helping to give my life meaning. Through them, I am getting to know myself better while realizing life is never truly lived unless you invest into the lives of others. They are also helping me fulfill my life's purpose and leaving a legacy of spiritually investing in the next generation so, we can fulfill our purpose in God's kingdom.

Throughout my life I have had many interests however, I most enjoy teaching the Bible, cooking and extending hospitality, listening, encouraging and praying with others. I enjoy the natural beauty around me and explore by going on walks and sky gazing. In my spare time, I enjoy spending time with family, going to church, reading, singing, meeting new friends, dancing, going to plays and the movies.

Made in the USA
San Bernardino, CA
13 December 2018